The Art & Science

SHUFFLE OFFENSES

FOR

MEN'S AND WOMEN'S

BASKETBALL

Harry L. "Mike" Harkins,
Grace Harkins
and Jerry Krause

COACHES
CHOICE

ISBN: 1-57167-272-9
Library of Congress Catalog Card Number: 98-88576

Book Layout: Janet Wahlfeldt
Cover Design: Julie L. Denzer
Cover Photos: Lipscomb University Sports Information Office
Production Manager: Michelle A. Summers

Coaches Choice Books is a division of: Sagamore Publishing, Inc.
                                           P.O. Box 647
                                           Champaign, IL 61824-0647
                                           Web Site: http//www.sagamorepub.com

DEDICATION

This book is dedicated to my wife, Grace, who, along with being the love of my life, has been a working partner in the books I have written. Without her meticulous efforts on the diagrams and hours spent typing, they might never have been completed.

—H. L. H.

This book is dedicated to all those who have been given unique talents to play the great game of basketball. May they acknowledge that gift by always giving something back to the game. May this basketball coaching series be a gift to basketball from the authors who have received so much from the sport.

—J. K.

ACKNOWLEDGMENTS

Harkins:

Grateful appreciation is expressed to the sources of my basketball knowledge, including: Russ Estey and Mike Krino, my high school coaches; Russ Beichly and Red Cochrane, my college coaches; Buck Hyser, who gave me my first coaching job; and the players who have played on my teams.

A final note of thanks goes to my children—Mike and his wife, Diane; Patti and her husband, Ric; and Jim and his wife, Jeanne—and my number-one fans, my grandchildren, Shellee, Jamee, Mike, Shawn, and Walker.

A special acknowledgment goes to Jerry Krause for his diligent efforts in helping me complete this book.

Krause:

It is much appreciated that I have been able to collaborate on these coaching books with my longtime coaching friend from the Great Northwest, Mike Harkins. I have long respected his knowledge of the game and his unique skill of making coaching ideas simple.

CONTENTS

Chapter

What This Book Will Do For You
Nine Shuffle Offenses For Men's and Women's Basketball

The shuffle offense constantly moves the defense to complicate its pressure and help assignments. The opposition's big defenders are forced to play some defense on the perimeter and the opposition's small players must, at times, guard their assigned offensive players in the pivot area. The shuffle offense's well-defined scoring options provide high-percentage shots.

This book offers nine shuffle offenses. To prevent these offenses from becoming too repetitive, pattern variation plays and pressure-relieving maneuvers are included. The pattern variation plays take the defenders' focus off the shuffle options by showing them something different—"a new picture." The pressure relievers are used to initiate the offense against strong defensive pressure and denial. They also provide other alternatives to the basic shuffle options when they are being anticipated and denied. At the close of each chapter are coaching tips. They vary from those that apply to all shuffle offenses to those that are specific to the shuffle offenses in the chapter. Also included are catch-up plays to be used when your point deficit is twice the number of minutes remaining on the game clock.

The chapters proceed in the following manner:

Chapter One—The triple-cut shuffle provides three basic options and a secondary crosscourt pass option.

Chapter Two—The big-player shuffle has a four-person basic motion around a talented big player.

Chapter Three—The wing-clear shuffle incorporates a unique two-option entry into its basic motion.

Chapter Four—The crisscross shuffle uses crossing post players to facilitate a three-option motion.

Chapter Five—The over-and-under shuffle utilizes the offside post player as the hub of its motion.

Chapter Six—The over-or-under shuffle keys on whether the first cutter goes over or under a double screen.

Chapter Seven—The double-down shuffle features a double-down screen.

Chapter Eight—The screen-and-roll shuffle uses the screen and roll in the midst of a shuffle pattern.

Chapter Nine—The "either-way" shuffle offers an alternative to reversing the ball.

Chapter Ten—Coaching tips for the shuffle offense help prepare the coach to teach the shuffle offense.

A coach may adopt one of these nine offenses as his/her basic motion or use one of the many plays that are offered to enhance a team's present offensive plan.

DIAGRAM KEY

OFFENSE

(1)   Offensive player

(1)   Offensive player with ball

(1)   (1) V cuts to get open

(1)   (1) up and out cuts to get open

★   Shot option

DEFENSE

X_1 Defender guarding Player #1

X_2 Defender guarding Player #2

X_3 Defender guarding Player #3

X_4 Defender guarding Player #4

X_5 Defender guarding Player #5

(2) - - -▶ **(1)**   Player #2 passes to player #1

(2) ∿∿∿▶   Player #2 dribbles

(1) ——▶   Player #1 cuts

(3) **(4)** - - -▶ **(2)**   Player (4) passes to (2) and screens fpr Player (3) who cuts

(2) ∿∿∿▶ **(4)**   Player (4) screens for player (2) who dribbles and then (4) rolls

CHAPTER 1

The Triple-Cut Shuffle

PERSONNEL

The Triple-Cut Shuffle has two groups of specialists. Players (1) and (5) are the jump shooters and players (2), (3), and (4) make the first cut to the low post and then post up. They also have an opportunity for a three-point shot via a crosscourt pass.

Also included in this chapter is an easily taught three-play, quick-shot series to be used at catch-up time.

THE BASIC MOTION FOR THE TRIPLE-CUT SHUFFLE

Diagram 1-1 shows the 1-3-1 set and point (1) make an entry pass to the weakside wing (2). This tells (3) to cut off (4) to the ballside low-post area. (4) then pops to the three-point wing to become a secondary option. (1) screens down for (5), who cuts to the ballside on the point. After screening for (5), (1) rolls to the ballside high post to become the third option.

Diagram 1-1: Triple-cut shuffle

If (3) or (1) are not open, (2) passes to (5) at the point, who reverses the ball to (4) and the triple-cut shuffle is repeated (see Diagrams 1-2 and 1-3).

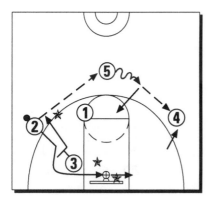

Diagram 1-2: Reverse

Diagram 1-3: Triple cut

Strongside Entry

When the entry pass from point (1) is made to the strongside wing (3), the low post (4) must hustle across the lane and stop to permit (2) to cut off (4)'s screen to the ballside post area (see Diagram 1-4).

**Diagram 1-4: Strongside Entry—
triple Cut**

From there, the triple-cut shuffle proceeds as before (see Diagrams 1-5 and 1-6).

Diagram 1-5: Triple Cut

Diagram 1-6: Reversal

PATTERN VARIATIONS

Reverse the Ball—Via the Middle Cutter

In Diagram 1-7, (4) passes to (5), the middle cutter, who has no shot so he/she turns to face the basket then passes to (2) at the offside wing.

This tells (4) to cut off (3), who steps out to screen and then pops to the wing (see Diagram 1-8).

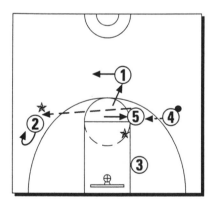

Diagram 1-7: Middle reversal

Diagram 1-8: First cut

(1) screens down for (5), who cuts to the point. (1) rolls to the ballside mid-post area, and the shuffle continues (see Diagram 1-9).

Diagram 1-9: Second, third cut

Reverse the Ball Via a Crosscourt Pass
In Diagram 1-10, (4) throws a crosscourt pass to (2), who cannot shoot. This tells (4) to cut off (3), who stepped out to screen and then popped to the wing.

(1) screens down for (5) and rolls to the mid-post area as the shuffle continues (see Diagram 1-11).

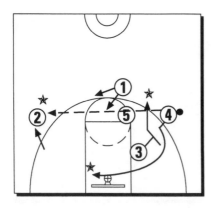

Diagram 1-10: Skip pass, first cut

Diagram 1-11: Second, third cut

The Two-Player Front Variation
When a coach desires to start the shuffle from a two-front guard, to take the pressure off a point guard and make the entry pass easier, the following method

may be used. In Diagram 1-12, (1) (the 2-1-2 set guard) passes to ballside forward (3). This tells the offside guard (2) to cut off post (5), who steps to that side to screen.

(1) screens down for (5), who cuts to the point. After screening, (2) rolls to the ballside high-post area (see Diagram 1-13).

Diagram 1-12: Two-guard entry— first cut

Diagram 1-13: Second and third cut

If neither (2) nor (1) is open, (3) passes to (5) and the triple-cut shuffle is run again (see Diagram 1-14).

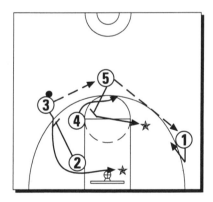

Diagram 1-14: Reversal to triple-cut

PRESSURE RELIEVERS
The Backdoor play
When defensive denial is strong, the cutter to the point may backdoor his/her defender and cut to the basket for a possible lob pass (see Diagram 1-15).

If (5) is not open, (3) replaces (5) at the point after the backdoor cut. (2) then passes to (3), who reverses the ball to (5) on the wing, and the shuffle is continued (see Diagram 1-16).

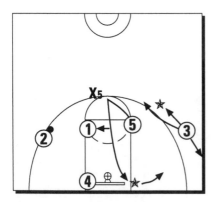

Diagram 1-15: Point overplay to backdoor

Diagram 1-16: Reversal to triple-cut

The triple-cut shuffle is an excellent plan to use during the main part of a game or when you are attempting to protect a lead at the game's end. However, the following quick-shot series should be used when your scoring deficit is double the minutes left on the clock. It is easy to teach and provides quick shots with new passes and little motion.

THE CATCH-UP OFFENSE

The Guard Clear Play (Play #1)
Diagram 1-17 shows point (1) bring the ball into the front court and pass to wing (2). (1) then cuts down the lane and loops around the offside post player (5). At this

Diagram 1-17: Guard clear entry

point, (2) and (4) play a two-on-two game, the offside wing (3) is responsible for defensive balance, and the clearout player (1) becomes the "dealer." The dealer may: (A) hustle back on defense with the offside wing, (B) attempt to intercept the opposition's outlet pass, (C) harass their rebounder, or (D) attempt to obtain an offensive rebound. The "dealer's" assignment should be made clear by the coach before a given game or situation.

THE TWO-ON-TWO PLAY

Once (1) has cleared the lane, (2) has the following options:

Option A
(2) can dribble off a screen by (4), who would then roll to the basket. (2) may shoot, hit (4) on the roll, pass to (5) posting up, or pass to (1) or (3) on the three-point perimeter (see Diagram 1-18) on a "penetrate and pitch" play.

If nothing develops, (1) comes to get the ball and the 1-3-1 pattern set is realigned.

Diagram 1-18: 2-on-2 pick and roll

Option B
(2) may also pass to (4) and make a "V" cut. (4) can then hand off to (2) and roll to the basket (see Diagram 1-19), or fake to (2) and dribble to the basket (see Diagram 1-20).

Either of these options results in a quick, high-percentage shot, a rebound triangle, good defensive balance and a chance to disrupt the opposition's potential fast break.

Diagram 1-19: Pass and "V" cut—handoff

Diagram 1-20: Pass and "V" cut—fake handoff and drive

The Wing-Clear Play (Play #2)

This play is Play #1 in disguise. (1) passes to (2) and makes an outside cut (2) returns the ball to (1) and clears over (4) and under (5). (1) and (4) use the same two-on-two options. Again, this play provides a quick, high-percentage shot, a rebound triangle, defensive balance, and a chance to disrupt their potential fast break (see Diagram 1-21).

The Backdoor Split (Play #3)

(1) notices strong defensive pressure on the wings so (1) bounce passes to (4) and (2) backdoors the defender on the wing (see Diagram 1-22).

Diagram 1-21: Handback 2-on-2

Diagram 1-22: High post to wing backdoor

If (2) is not open on the backdoor, a "V" cut is made on a popout cut to the defender off of (1), who followed the entry pass and cut toward (2). (4) passes to (2) for a shot or picks for (2) and rolls (see Diagrams 1-23 and 1-24) or fakes to (2) and takes the ball inside (see Diagram 1-25). Note that, in either case, (1) had cleared across the lane and looped around (5) to become the "dealer."

Diagram 1-23

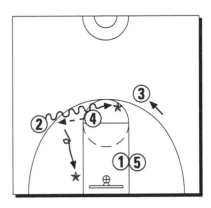

Diagram 1-24

Diagram 1-25

In either case, the team maintained the same previously mentioned offensive fundamentals.

Note: In all these examples, high post (4) lined up on (2)'s side of the court. In reality, (4) is instructed to set-up on (3)'s side half the time. Strong rebounder (5) always lines up on the opposite side from high post (4).

COACHING TIPS FOR THE TRIPLE-CUT SHUFFLE

Strategy
The shuffle and the catch-up offense *may* be used together throughout the game. However, the shuffle *should* be used to kill the clock and the catch-up offense *should* be used at "catch-up time" when your point deficit is double the amount of minutes left on the clock.

When your team has better athletes than the opposition, the catch-up plan is preferable. When your opponent has the superior players, make them play defense by running a disciplined shuffle pattern.

If your team lacks a strong point guard, run a two-pattern set (pre-shuffle) play to get into the shuffle easier.

Put your best jump shooters in the (1) and (5) positions and teach them to catch the ball in a jump stop all-purpose position, triple-threat stance.

The inside players ((2), (3), and (4)) must practice their pivot moves. Pivot shots lead to more opportunities for second shots, more fouls on the opposition, and they are high-percentage shots.

Teams will attempt to deny the shuffle's reversal so teach the pressure relievers early and keep them sharp by regular review.

All shuffles are repetitive, so use pattern variations to present new "pictures" to opposition defenses.

Throw the crosscourt pass ball reversal in the first half. This will help unclog the middle and facilitate the three basic shuffle options. Teach the player receiving the crosscourt pass that, if pressured, he or she has room to drive to the baseline.

CHAPTER 2

The Big-Player Shuffle

PERSONNEL

This shuffle is for a team that has a talented post player and wants to run a motion offense. It is designed to provide functional movement that will challenge the four perimeter defenders. This will permit post (5) to operate one-on-one in the lane with a minimum of defensive help clogging the middle. The ideal personnel would be four mobile perimeter players and a talented post player. This post player need not be bigger than other players but must be proficient at scoring and passing from inside.

THE BIG-PLAYER SHUFFLE MOTION

The Basic Four-Player Shuffle Motion

Diagram 2-1 shows (1) pass to wing (2). This keys (3) to cut low off (4), who stepped out to screen and then popped to the three-point area to become a possible scoring option. (1) moves down to screen for (4). (At this time, (5) is not shown as part of the offense.)

If (3) is not open on the shuffle cut at the basket, the cut is continued to a position halfway between the lane line and the three-point line (the short corner). (1) continues down to screen for (4), who cuts to the point. After screening, (1) pops to a position behind the three-point line (see Diagram 2-2).

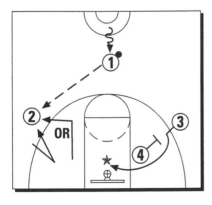

Diagram 2-1: Big-shuffle entry

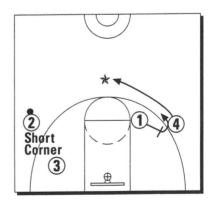

Diagram 2-2: Big shuffle

(2) looks first for (3) and then to (1) in the three-point area. If they are not open, (2) passes to (4) at the point, who can shoot or (as shown in Diagram 2-3) reverse the ball to (1) and key a repeat of the four-player shuffle motion (see Diagram 2-4).

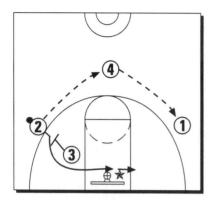

Diagram 2-3: Reversal

Diagram 2-4: Four player— shuffle

The Post Options

A. Post (5) may swing to the ballside at anytime. Diagrams 2-5 and 2-6 show the shuffle in motion and (5) coming to the ballside in the medium/high post area.

Diagram 2-5: Post to ball, shuffle cutter to short corner

Diagram 2-6:Post to ball

Note that the first cutter, upon not receiving the ball from the wing, clears one-halfway between the lane line and the three-point line to the short corner. This gives post (5) room to work if he/she receives a pass from the wing.

B. Post (5) may also cut away from the ball. This tells the first cutter to cut high using (5) as a screener and then post up back to the ball (see Diagram 2-7).

(2) attempts to get the ball to (3) as (5) doubles back to the high-post area (two cutters per screen). (1) screens away for (4) and then pops outside the three-point line (see Diagram 2-8).

Diagram 2-7: High first cut

Diagram 2-8: Second (post)and third (point) cut

(2) may then pass to (3) in the post, to (5) doubling back in the high post, to (1) for a trey, or to (4) at the point to continue the shuffle. When (2) passes to (5), (5) may shoot or pass to (3) inside the fronting defender (see Diagram 2-9).

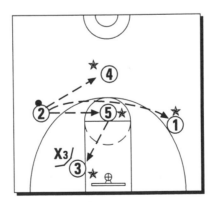

Diagram 2-9: Wing options

Diagrams 2-10 through 2-13 show (5) executing those options.

Diagram 2-10: (5) to the ball (high post)

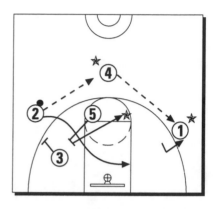

Diagram 2-11: (5) screen away from the ball (Part A)

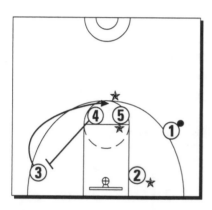

Diagram 2-12: (5) away from the ball (Part B) and cut back to the high post

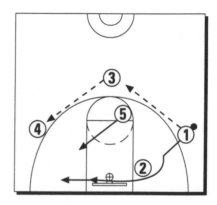

Diagram 2-13: (5) to the ball

PATTERN VARIATIONS

Variation #1: Screen the Hedger

When the opposition is hedging to stop the first high cut over (5) in Option B, a lob option may be added for (5). Diagram 2-14 shows (1) pass to (2), (5) screen away, and (3) cut over (5).

Seeing that X5 stepped out to stop (3)'s cut, (4) moves up to screen the hedger (X5). (5) uses (4)'s screen to cut to the offside lay-up area for a possible lob pass from (2). (see Diagram 2-15).

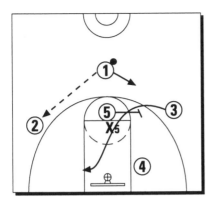

Diagram 2-14: Wing entry

Diagram 2-15: Screen the hedger

Seeing that the lob play has been keyed by (4), (1) V cuts back to the point. If the lob does not open up, (2) passes to (1) and the team returns to its original pattern set from which a new shuffle sequence may be run. (see Diagram 2-16).

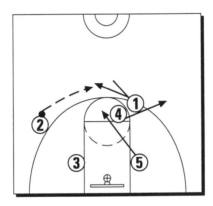

Diagram 2-16

Variation #2: Two to One

If a team wants to run the shuffle from a two-guard front, the shuffle cross works well with the big player shuffle. Diagram 2-17 shows (1) pass to forward (3) and cut over post (5) to screen away for forward (4), who cuts to the point. The other guard (2) uses (1)'s cut and a definite screen by (5) to cut to the ballside low-post area. If (2) is not open, he/she clears toward (3) in the three-point area. (5) may then: (A) stay put and the shuffle cross will be repeated; (B) come to the ball and post; or (C) cut away from the ball to screen for (3).

Option A

(5) Stays

Diagrams 2-17 through 2-19 shows (5) staying in the middle of the lane and keying a repeat of the shuffle cross.

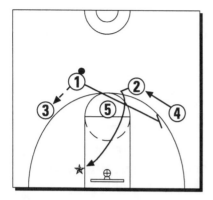

Diagram 2-17: The shuffle cross entry from two-guard front

Diagram 2-18: Reverse and reset

Diagram 2-19: Repeat the shuffle cross

Note that (5) cuts to the ball after the second shuffle cross.

Option B

(5) Cuts to the Ball

In Diagrams 2-20 and 2-21, (5) cuts to the ball after the shuffle cross is concluded.

Diagram 2-20: Shuffle cross entry

Diagram 2-21: (5) cut to ball

Note that (2) cleared the post area for (5) and that (1) popped wide to become a three-point option.

If (2) is not open on the first cut, (3) could not get the ball to (5) in the post, and (1) is not open for a three-point shot, (3) passes to (4) and the shuffle continues (see Diagram 2-22).

Diagram 2-22: Reversal

Option C

(5) Cuts Away

When (5) cuts away from the ball, the guard in the low post (2) must not clear across the lane.

Diagram 2-23 shows the shuffle cross entry. Diagram 2-24 shows (5) cut away and (2) also move to the other side.

Diagram 2-23: Shuffle cross-entry

Diagram 2-24: (5) Cut away

Diagram 2-25 shows (3) pass to (5) and (5) pass to (1) inside on a seal move.

Diagram 2-25: (5) Cut away and flash back

Variation #3: Feed-the-Post Play

When post (5) can clearly dominate the defender, the feed-the-post play may be used. Diagram 2-26 shows (1) dribble at the wing on the low post's side. This clears (3) to loop around (4) and (5) to the point. At the same time, (4) screens for (5), who cuts to the midpost area. (4) rolls to the offside post.

If (1) cannot get the ball to (5), the pass is made to (3) at the point, who also looks inside to (5) on a seal. If (5) is not open, (3) reverses the ball to (2). This tells (4) to screen for (5), and (3) to screen for (1) (see Diagram 2-27).

Diagram 2-26: Dribble entry to wing clear

Diagram 2-27: Reversal

This process is repeated until (5) receives a pass and makes a one-on-one play, or a perimeter jump shot opens up.

PRESSURE RELIEVER

The Dribble-Entry Lob

When (1) is having trouble making an entry pass to a wing, a dribble entry is made at a wing (as at (2) in Diagram 2-28) which clears the wing over (5), who moves over to screen. If (2) is not open for the lob pass, the cutter continues to the offside wing. (1) then passes to (3), who moved to the point. (3) passes to (2) and the shuffle is in motion (see Diagrams 2-29, 2-30 and 2-31).

Diagram 2-28: Dribble entry lob

Diagram 2-29: Reversal

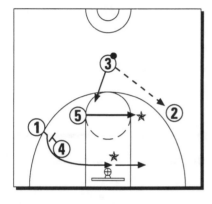

Diagram 2-30: Big-player shuffle

Diagram 2-31: Second and third cut

If the dribble entry for the lob play is made on the weakside, the player in the low-post position (4) must join (5) in a cut to the ballside (see Diagrams 2-32 through 2-34).

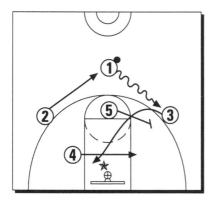

Diagram 2-32: Dribble entry lob to weakside

Diagram 2-33: Big shuffle

Diagram 2-34: Second and third cutter—big shuffle

(5) and (4) cut to the ball. The shuffle is keyed on the reversal. (5) cuts to the ball.

COACHING TIPS FOR THE BIG-PLAYER SHUFFLE

Spacing and Motion
If the perimeter shuffle cutters will stay wide, maintain the motion at the correct tempo, and take their open shots, (5) will have room enough to utilize pivot skills especially in the medium/high post.

The Scoring Options
The first cutter (3) in Diagram 2-35, should be under control and well balanced by the time he/she is under the basket. The passer (2) should attempt to get the cutter the ball at that time. If the pass is not made, the first cutter (3) must clear the lane to the short corner to make room for the talented post (5) to swing to the ballside.

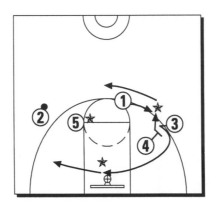

Diagram 2-35: Big shuffle

The second cutter (4) (who will cut to the point) should have popped to the three-point area after screening for the first cutter (3).

This move by (4) gives the offense an extra option and spreads the defense.

(5) should use a jump stop after cutting to the ballside post, assume a wide stance with both hands up, and provide a target hand away from the defender. When catching the ball, be aware of the defender's location and have an appropriate move to gain an advantage.

The second cutter (5) must arrive at the point when the passer (2) is ready. (5) should catch the ball in a position to square up and shoot, reverse the ball to the opposite wing, and, if really pressured, to pivot and/or dribble drive to the basket.

The four shuffle cutters must be willing to turn the offense over until a high-percentage shot develops. In general, defensive pressure tends to subside with each pass.

CHAPTER 3

The Wing-Clear Shuffle

PERSONNEL

The wing-clear shuffle offense is also designed for mobile players with all-around skills.

THE BASIC MOTION FOR THE WING-CLEAR SHUFFLE

Diagram 3-1 shows point (1) dribble to (2)'s side of the court. This tells (2) to clear over the top of (4) and across the lane. (4) uses (2)'s cut to get open to cut to a high wing position. (1) passes to (4) and (2) screens for (3) on the far side of the lane. (3) cuts to the ballside. (1) hesitates and screens down for (5), who cuts to the point. (see Diagram 3-2).

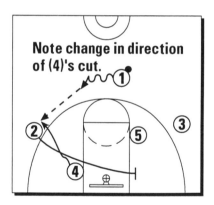

Diagram 3-1: Wing clear entry

Diagram 3-2: Wing clear shuffle

If (3) is not open, (4) passes to (5), as (2) cuts to the wing area. The team is now back in a 1-4 set. (see Diagram 3-3).

(5) keys the motion by dribbling to one side (as to (2)'s side in Diagram 3-4). This tells

Diagram 3-3: Reset

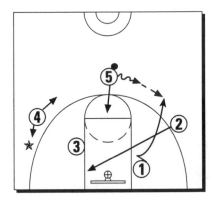

Diagram 3-4: Entry

(2) to screen for (1) and cut through and across the lane. The wing-clear shuffle is repeated (see Diagram 3-5).

Wing (1) must also be aware of the wing teammate in the far three-point area.

Diagram 3-5: Wing clear shuffle

SHUFFLE VARIATIONS

Screen and Roll
When the ball is at the point, either before the original entry pass has been made or while the pattern is in progress, a quick screen-and-roll play may be run. In Diagram 3-6, (1) has the ball at the point, as wing (2) makes a clearout cut over (4) and across the lane.

This time, however, (4), instead of popping to the high wing, moves up to screen (1)'s defender. (1) uses this screen to attempt to penetrate for a jump shot or all the way to the basket. (4) rolls to the basket (see Diagram 3 -7).

Diagram 3-6: Wing clear over the top

Diagram 3-7: High screen and roll

If neither (1) nor (4) is open, (4) clears across the lane and under, as (5) sets a definite screen on (3)'s defender. (3) is taught to cut over (5) and (2) as soon as (4) clears. It also helps if (1) maintains the dribble until (3) cuts (see Diagram 3-8).

If (3) is not open, (4) loops to the point and receives a pass from (1) and (2) pops to the wing (see Diagram 3-9).

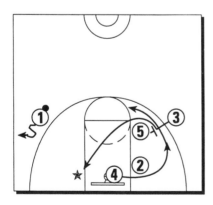

Diagram 3-8: High shuffle cut

Diagram 3-9: Reversal

(4) dribbles toward (1)'s side and (1) keys the shuffle (or another screen and roll) by clearing over (3) and to the offside low-post area (see Diagram 3-10).

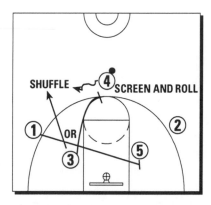

Diagram 3-10: Wing-clear entry over-the-top

In general, the key elements of timing for the screen-and-roll play are: (a) the point must maintain the dribble as long as possible; (b) (4), the screener, should screen, roll, clear, and hustle to the point; and (c) (3), the offside wing, must cut over the double screen when (4) clears the lane (see Diagrams 3-11 and 3-12).

Diagram 3-11: High screen and roll (after reset)

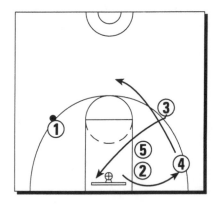

Diagram 3-12: High shuffle cut

If point (1) penetrates and can't shoot, (4) must come to the ball and take it back to the point where a new play may be keyed (see Diagram 3-13).

Diagram 3-13: Reset

The Two-Guard Front
When a coach desires to use a two-guard front, either from necessity or to have more variety in his offense, he/she can use this pattern set play.

The two guards ((1) and (2) in Diagram 3-14) bring the ball into the front court and a guard-to-guard pass is made. The passing guard (1) then cuts down the lane where (4) and (5) are in the post positions and (3) is stacked under (4).

(1) then has two options: (A) cut around (5) to the wing on the single side. (3) always cuts to the wing opposite (1), so (3) cuts to the wing on (4)'s side (see Diagram 3-15).

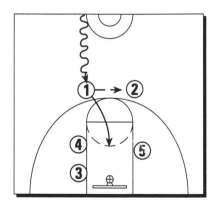

Diagram 3-14: Guard through

Diagram 3-15: Use single screen

Or (B) (1) may cut around (4) and (3) on the double side. This tells (3) to cross the lane and pop to the wing on (5)'s side (see Diagram 3-16).

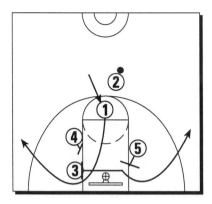

Diagram 3-16: Use double screen

In either case, (2) then passes to a wing and screens away for the other wing. The ballside post also screens away for the other post (see Diagram 3-17).

From there, (1) passes to (3) and starts the shuffle motion (see Diagram 3-18).

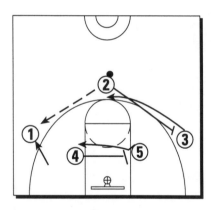

Diagram 3-17: Screen away

Diagram 3-18: Wing clear shuffle

These pattern sets (pre-shuffle variations) have a definite function. Shuffle patterns are very repetitive, and smart defensive players can sometimes anticipate the next pass and step into the passing lane for an interception. These plays give the opposition a new "picture" and make their defensive jobs more difficult.

PRESSURE RELIEVERS

The Dribble-Clear Wing-Cross Play

When defensive pressure is making it difficult to execute a point-to-wing pass, (1) dribbles into the front court on a side and directly at a wing (as at (2) in Diagram 3-19). This tells (2) to clear across the lane and set a screen for the offside wing (3). At the same time, (4) moves across the lane to a position next to (5).

Diagram 3-19: Wing cross

(4) and (5) then screen down for (2), who loops to the point (see Diagram 3-20).

(4) loops around (5) to the wing, (5) posts up, and another shuffle sequence is keyed as wing (1) passes to (2) and clears (see Diagram 3-21).

Diagram 3-20: Double down

Diagram 3-21: Reset to wing clear shuffle

COACHING TIPS FOR THE WING-CLEAR SHUFFLE TIMING

When the entry pass is made to start the shuffle, the receiver (4) in Diagram 3-22) should use a jump stop, catch the ball, and then make a jab step toward the baseline. This is necessary because it backs up (4)'s defender and helps give the clearing wing (2) time to get across the lane and set the screen for (3). This baseline threat by (4) and the fact that (3) makes a wide, slow change of pace before exiting, allows (2) time to stop before the screen occurs and helps avoid a moving screen foul by (2).

Diagram 3-22: Entry and first cut

Spacing
The three-point line should be used as a spacing device. The wing players stay outside the three-point line and free-throw line high. The point stays above the three-point line to make the entry pass. Staying wide in this manner spreads the defense and makes their conversions from pressure to help and recover more difficult. For years, coaches who use motion offenses have told their teams not to flatten out the offense and now they have the three-point line to use as a boundary line to enhance that principle.

Three-Point Attempts
The player with the ball must learn to be aware of teammates located outside the three-point line. This is especially true after a dribble penetration or receiving a pass in the lane. The number of team three-point attempts to be taken and attempts by a particular individual should be made clear by the coach during practice. Teach players to learn to use their strengths.

Individual Techniques
If the point will declare to a particular side, the wing on that side will know who must cut over the post to form a natural screen and initiate the shuffle. The post will then brush the clearout cutter on the way to the high wing or move directly out to screen for the point.

The second cutter must time the cut to the point. If too early, he/she should delay the cut by doubling back a couple of steps and then coming to the point.

CHAPTER 4

The Crisscross Shuffle

PERSONNEL

This shuffle is for a team of mobile players who lack "post-up" ability. The post, (4) and (5), are used as screeners until they become part of the perimeter shuffle motion. This is a great offense to use versus a defensive team that has big, slow players.

THE BASIC CRISSCROSS SHUFFLE MOTION

The two primary entries that are used to start this offense are an integral part of this shuffle plan. It starts in a set that has a point and a double stack. Point (1) brings the ball to the head of the key and then toward a side. In Diagram 4-1, (1) dribbles to the side on which (5) and (3) form the stack. This tells (3) to cut up to the now offside-guard position. (1) must maintain the dribble. (3) can get to the front by: (A) looping around (4) and (2)'s stack (see Diagram 4-1), or (B) faking the looping move around (4) and (5), then cutting up the middle and back toward (1) (see Diagram 4-2).

Diagram 4-1: Entry—loop cut

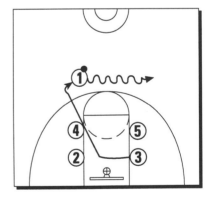

Diagram 4-2: Entry—middle cut

Note: If (1) had dribbles to (2)'s side, (2) would have cut to the offside-guard area opposite (1).

(1) passes to the now offside guard (3), who reverses the ball to (2), popping out of (5)'s downscreen (see Diagram 4-3).

(4) then steps up to blindscreen for (3), who cuts to the basket for a possible lob pass, and then clears. Post (5) then crosses the lane behind (4) (see Diagram 4-4).

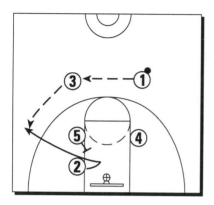

Diagram 4-3: G-G-F entry

Diagram 4-4: Crisscross

(1) cuts off (5)'s screen to the ballside low-post area (see Diagram 4-5).

After (1)'s cut, (4) and (5) screen down for (3), who cuts to the ballside of the point (see Diagram 4-6).

Diagram 4-5: First cut

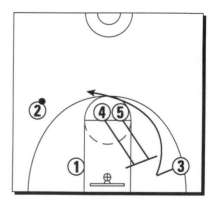

Diagram 4-6: Second cut using double down

Once all the options have been explored and (3) has the ball at the point, (2) stacks with (1), and (4) stacks under (5) (see Diagram 4-7).

Diagram 4-7: Restack

(3) can then dribble to either side and repeat the three scoring options that comprise the crisscross shuffle (see Diagrams 4-8 through 4-11).

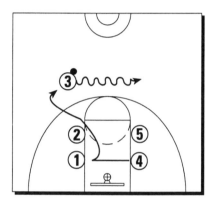

Diagram 4-8: Entry for crisscross shuffle

Diagram 4-9: G-G-F Entry— crisscross cut #1

Diagram 4-10: Crisscross cut #2

Diagram 4-11: Double down

PATTERN VARIATION

The Double Down Three-Point Variation

At the juncture in the pattern where the double screen down occurs, a three-point variation may be used. Diagram 4-12 shows (4) and (5) moving down to screen for (3). This time, however, once they are inside the free-throw line, the inside screener (5) in Diagram 4-12) loops over (4) to the three-point area. (3) helps (5) get open by setting a screen on (5)'s defender. If (5) is open, (2) passes for a three-point attempt.

After screening, (3) pops to the ballside head of the key. If (5) is not open, (2) passes to (3) and a new play sequence is organized as the double stacks are reformed (see Diagram 4-13).

(3) may then dribble to either side to start the shuffle.

Diagram 4-12: Trey flare for inside player on double down

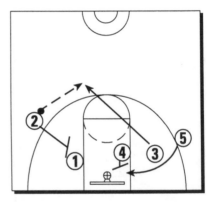

Diagram 4-13: Reset into double stack

PRESSURE RELIEVERS

The Clear Out

When (3) in Diagram 4-14 arrives at the guard position and cannot receive a pass due to defensive pressure, (3) clears down the lane and (4) steps out front.

(1) passes to (4) and the pattern continues (see Diagram 4-15).

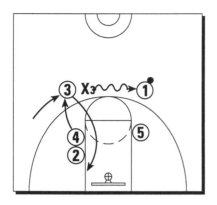

Diagram 4-14: G-G Overplay and backout

Diagram 4-15: Crisscross shuffle

The Screen-and-Roll Play

This play is run when (1) cannot pass to the cutter out front (after (1) has dribbled to the side). Diagram 4-16 shows (3) come out front and be unable to receive the pass. This keys the post on (1)'s side to step up to backscreen for the ballhandler.

(1) dribbles off (5)'s screen and (5) rolls to the basket. (1) can shoot or hit (5) on the roll. This play is one reason (1) must maintain the dribble (see Diagram 4-17).

Diagram 4-16

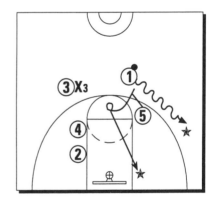

Diagram 4-17: Screen and roll

This screen-and-roll play may be used after, or in place of, the clearout play shown previously. If no shot results, a reset into the double stack is made.

Pass to the Post

As (1) brings the ball into the front court and sees that the wings, (2) and (3), are already out of their stacks, the ballside wing (2) then loops around the post (4). This tells the post (4) to break high and receive a bounce pass from (1) (see Diagram 4-18).

(3) cuts off (5) to the lay-up area and then across the lane. (see Diagram 4-19).

Diagram 4-18: Wing Loop

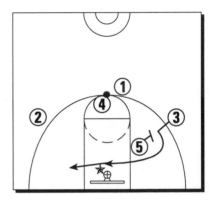

Diagram 4-19

(5) then steps up to screen for (1), who flares out to the three-point area as (5) rolls down the lane (see Diagram 4-20).

If no one is open, (4) gives the ball to (2), and the basic offense is reset (see Diagram 4-21).

Diagram 4-20: Point flare

Diagram 4-21: Reset into double stack

COACHING TIPS FOR THE CRISSCROSS SHUFFLE

Handling Defensive Pressure
This offense is very dependent on the guard-to-guard pass that is made once the point has dribbled to a side. When it is being denied, the pressure relievers must be run. The coach must first decide which one(s) to include and then work on them

extensively. Coaches should insist that (1) maintains the dribble until utilizing a pressure reliever if the guard-to-guard pass is denied. To repeat, the three pressure release choices are:

The Clear Out (see Diagrams 4-22 and 4-23).

Diagram 4-22: Lone backcut

Diagram 4-23: Entry—crisscross shuffle

The Screen and Roll (see Diagram 4-24).

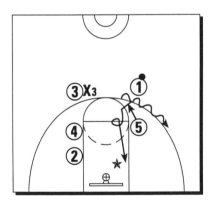

Diagram 4-24: Screen and roll by single post

The Pass to the Post (see Diagrams 4-25 and 4-26).

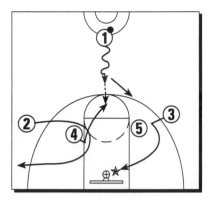

Diagram 4-25: Post pass after wing loop

Diagram 4-26: Point flare

CHAPTER 5

The Under-and-Over Shuffle

PERSONNEL

The over-and-under shuffle offense is also designed for mobile players with all-around skills.

THE BASIC MOTION UNDER-AND-OVER SHUFFLE

This shuffle begins as (1) passes to a wing (as to (2) in Diagram 5-1). This tells the ballside post (4) to clear across the lane and *under* offside post (5). At the same time, the offside wing (3) makes a change of direction and cuts *over* (5).

(1) then comes down and screens for (5), who cuts to the point. If (2) cannot pass to (3), he/she passes to (5) at the point (see Diagram 5-2).

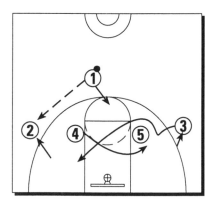

Diagram 5-1: Entry and high shuffle—under and over

Diagram 5-2: Reversal

(5) passes to (4), and the pattern is repeated (see Diagrams 5-3 and 5-4).

If (2) is a strong post up player, (4) should take more time in the attempt to get the ball inside.

Diagram 5-3: Entry-under and over

Diagram 5-4: Third cut

PATTERN VARIATIONS

Variation #1: The Corner Play

During the running of the shuffle, the ballside post (4) in Diagram 5-5) usually clears to the off-side wing on a point-to-wing entry pass.

To call the corner play, (4) (instead of clearing to the offside wing area) cuts to the ballside corner and calls out "corner." At the same time, (3) cuts over (5) to the ballside medium post area (see Diagram 5-6).

Diagram 5-5: Entry and over— under

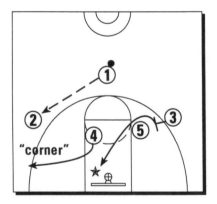

Diagram 5-6: Corner call

(2) checks (3)'s cut and, if not open, passes to (4) in the corner and cuts over (3), who steps out to screen (see Diagram 5-7).

If (4) cannot pass to (2), (4) dribbles to the wing and (1) screens down for (5), who pops to the point. (2) completes the cut to the offside wing (see Diagram 5-8).

Diagram 5-7: Corner pass and shuffle away

Diagram 5-8: Second cut

(4) passes to (5) at the point, who reverses it to (2). From there, the under-and-over shuffle resumes (see Diagrams 5-9 and 5-10).

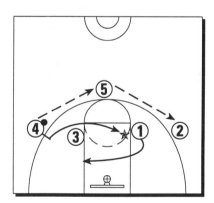

Diagram 5-9: Reversal to under-and-over shuffle

Diagram 5-10: Under-and-over shuffle

This corner play permits the team to interject a variation into the pattern with an easy-to-read key, and then smoothly return to the shuffle.

Variation #2: The Lob Option

The lob option is another maneuver that may be inserted into the under-and-over shuffle without disturbing the flow of the pattern.

Diagram 5-11 shows the pattern at a juncture where post (5) is at the point position and has made a pass to (2) at the wing. This keyed the ballside post (4) to clear across the lane under the opposite post and the offside wing (3) to cut over post (1) to the ballside. Ordinarily, (5), at the point, would now come down and screen for (1), who would cut to the point. However, in this case, with post (5) at the point, (1) moves up and screens for (5), who cuts to the offside lay-up area for a possible lob pass (see Diagram 5-12).

Diagram 5-11: Over and under

Diagram 5-12: Backscreen post for lob option

If (2) cannot lob to (5), (1) steps to the point, receives a pass from (2), and reverses the ball to (4) as the pattern continues (see Diagrams 5-13 and 5-14).

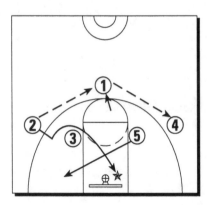

Diagram 5-13: Reversal to under-and-over shuffle

Diagram 5-14: Under-and-over shuffle

This variation of the pattern must be run in practice until it becomes automatic. The coach should point out that the key is when post (5) is at the point. He/she should also stress that (5)'s defender may be a less than agile tall player and that (5) makes an excellent target for a lob pass.

Variation #3: The Perimeter Check Play
If the team has adequate three-point shooters and defenses are jamming the middle to stop the shuffle, this perimeter-oriented play may be run.

In Diagram 5-15, (1) bounce passes to post (4), who is a strong one-on-one player. (1) cuts off post (5) and then (5) pops to the perimeter. If (1) is not open, (1) loops around (3) on the downscreen and then (3) moves back to the perimeter. Wing (2) then makes perimeter clear cut along the baseline to open the side for (4) (see Diagram 5-16).

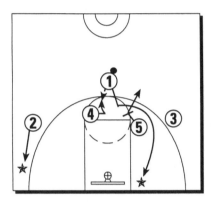

Diagram 5-15: High post entry-backscreen

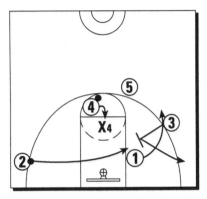

Diagram 5-16: Wing clear cut

makes a (4) turns to face the basket for a one-on-one play with the defender now having no defensive help. As (4) penetrates, the perimeter players (especially (5)) move to improve their spacing. (4) can shoot or pass to any open teammate for a three-point shot. If nothing develops, (1) comes to get the ball and the team reorganizes into its 1-4 pattern set.

PRESSURE RELIEVERS

The Dribble-Entry Lob Play
When (1) is having trouble making the entry pass, a dribble entry is made to clear the wing ((2) in Diagram 5-17) across the lane and under the offside post (5). At the same time, the offside wing (3) cuts over (5).

(3) moves a step toward the corner and (4) loops across the lane to screen for (5). (5) fakes a cut to the basket and uses (4)'s screen to move to the point (see Diagram 5-18).

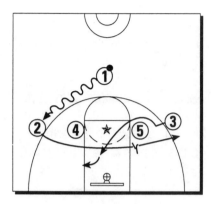

Diagram 5-17: Dribble entry—wing clear opposite

Diagram 5-18

(4) then rearpivots into the lane, using a wide stance, and may receive a lob pass from (1). (1) should maintain the dribble as long as possible since he/she is the feeder for this entire play (see Diagram 5-19).

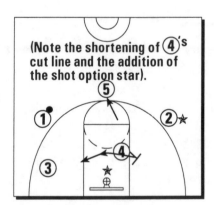

Diagram 5-19: Post lob look

If neither (3) nor (4) are open, (1) passes to (5) at the point and the under-and-over shuffle pattern is executed (see Diagrams 5-20 and 5-21).

Diagram 5-20: Under-and-over shuffle

Diagram 5-21: Completion

Note in Diagram 5-20 that (5) was pressured so he/she faked a cut to the basket and came back to the point, and received the pass from (1). The Shuffle then continues as shown in Diagram 5-21.

Anytime the ball is at the wing, a skip pass to the other wing for three is also an option.

Backdoor Entry
When a wing is unable to get open for an entry pass (see (2) in Diagram 5-22), the post on that side (4) steps out and receives a pass from (1). This tells (2) to backdoor the defender.

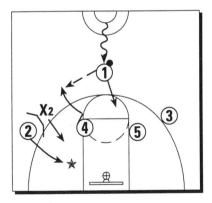

Diagram 5-22: Post pass

If (2) is not open, (2) continues across the lane and cuts under (5) as (3) cuts over the top and the pattern continues (see Diagrams 5-23 and 5-24).

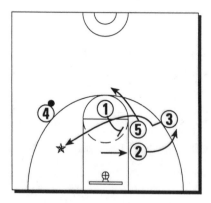

Diagram 5-23: Reversal

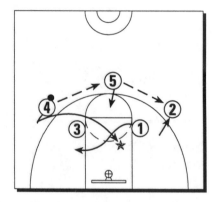

Diagram 5-24: Reversal to under-and-over shuffle

COACHING TIPS FOR THE UNDER-AND-OVER SHUFFLE

Timing

When the initial entry pass is made to a wing, the onside post ((4) in Diagram 5-25) must clear immediately and the cutting wing must time the cut to be going over (5) as (4) is coming under.

(1) hesitates and then screens down for (5), who cuts to the point. (5) should not be too early because it invites defensive overplay. This might involve a hesitation or change of direction on the cut to the point (see Diagram 5-26).

Diagram 5-25: Under and over

Diagram 5-26: Cut to the point

Depth for the Offense

This pattern, as with all shuffle patterns, is very repetitious. This can enable smart defenders to anticipate and cause disruptions. Therefore, the variations and pressure relievers must be incorporated into the offensive plan early in the season. How many and which ones to be included are questions that must be answered by the coach who evaluates the experiences, learning rate, and effectiveness of the team and it's offense.

CHAPTER 6

The Over-or-Under Shuffle

PERSONNEL

This shuffle is designed for five mobile players. However, it can be adjusted when run with the UCLA plays to accommodate a talented post player keeping him/her in the post area.

THE BASIC MOTION OVER-OR-UNDER SHUFFLE

Point (1) begins this pattern by passing to a wing (as to (2) in Diagram 6-1). This keys the ballside post (4) to move across the lane and set up above the offside post (5). (3) then cuts off the double screen over or under.

The Cut Over

When (3) chooses to cut over the top of (4) and (5), it keys the following motion. Point (1) comes down and screens for the top player of the double screen (4), who cuts to the point. (see Diagram 6 -2).

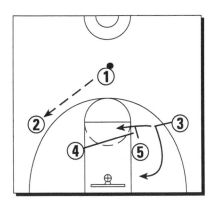

Diagram 6-1: Entry pass

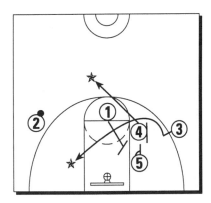

Diagram 6-2: Cut over

(1) continues the cut down the lane and loops around (5) to the wing, and the shuffle cuts may be repeated once (5) swings to the ballside top of the key and the ball is reversed to (1) via (4) (see Diagrams 6-3 and 6-4).

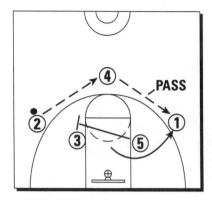

Diagram 6-3: Reversal

Diagram 6-4: Over or under

(2) may then cut over or under the double screen.

The Cut Under
This time, (2) chooses to cut under the double screen. This tells the point (4) to screen for the bottom player of the wall (See Diagrams 6-5 and 6-6).

Diagram 6-5: Under cut

Diagram 6-6: Point screen low

(3) cuts to the point. (4) then loops around (5) to the wing and (5) swings to the ballside top of the double screen. From there, a new offensive sequence may be run (see Diagram 6-7).

Diagram 6-7: Reset into over-or-under shuffle

The key to remember is that if the wing cutter goes over the top of the wall, the top screener of the wall will be screened for and will cut to the point. If the wing cutter goes under the wall, the bottom screener will be screened for and will cut to the point. This variety makes it much more difficult for the defense than a standard shuffle.

PATTERN VARIATIONS

Variation #1: The UCLA Shuffle Mix
Another way to run this shuffle is to combine it with the UCLA plays. The pattern set play for this offense begins when point (1) passes to a wing (as to (4) in Diagram 6-8) and cuts down the lane to set up in the low-post area. From this set, (4) may key one of three plays: The UCLA Downscreen, the screen and roll, or the over-or-under shuffle. Note that (3) moved to a position above the lane line on the side. (3) may also receive a pass from (2) for a one-on-one play.

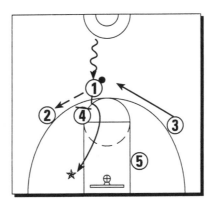

Diagram 6-8: UCLA shuffle cut

The UCLA Downscreen
After (1) has made the shuffle cut, (4) steps out to the head of the key and receives a pass from (2), who then downscreens for (1), who pops to the wing. (4) may then pass to (1) at the wing, or to (2) or (5) in the low posts. If (3)'s defender drops off to help, he/she becomes a three-point option (see Diagram 6-9).

Diagram 6-9: Popout

The Screen-and-Roll Play
This time, post (4) (after (1) passes to (2) and shuffle cuts to the low-post area) moves over to screen for (2). This tells (1) to clear the low-post area by moving across the lane and looping around (5) to the offside-wing position (See Diagram 6-10).

(2) dribbles off (4), who rolls to the basket. (2) may then shoot, hit (4) on the roll, pass to (1) in the three-point area, or pass to (5) posting up on a "muscle post" move (see Diagram 6-11).

Diagram 6-10: Screen-and-roll

Diagram 6-11: Screen-and-roll, muscle post

The Over-or-Under Shuffle

(4)'s key for the regular shuffle is to stay in the post and raise both hands. This tells (2) to take a dribble toward (3), who comes to meet the pass. Note that (5) cuts to the wing (see Diagram 6-12).

From there, the pattern may be run in either of two ways. (A) It may be run with the regular over or under options. First cutter (2) may cut over or under the double screen. This will often result in a different high post each time the offense is turned over (see Diagram 6-13).

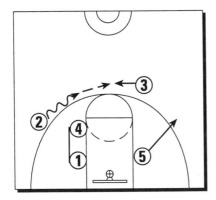

Diagram 6-12

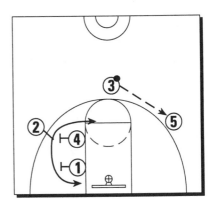

Diagram 6-13: Over or under

(B) (4) may be kept in the high post by insisting that the first cutter always cuts low off the double screen (see Diagram 6-14).

This method keeps (4) in the high post and allows (4) to call any of the three plays each time the offense is turned over (see Diagram 6-15).

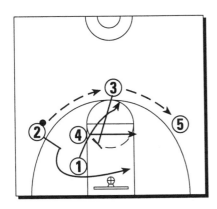

Diagram 6-14: Under-permanent post

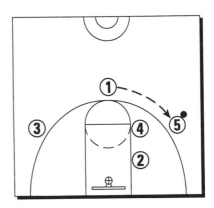

Diagram 6-15: Reversal

(4) may receive a pass and shoot, step out to the point to receive a pass and call the downscreen, move over to screen for (5), or stand still and raise both arms to call the shuffle. Constantly changing post players as in method (A), is much harder to teach and execute than method (B) but can present more problems for the defense.

These UCLA plays also come in handy for a shuffle team when they are trailing and time is running out. They can be run at that time with a strong emphasis on the three-point perimeter options.

Variation #2: The Pre-Pattern Lob Play

To add variety to the shuffle offense, a pre-pattern lob play may be added. As (1) dribbles up to the head of the key, a post ((5) in Diagram 6-16) moves up to the high post. Seeing this, (1) passes to the wing opposite (5) and cuts off (5) to the lay-up area for a possible lob pass. Note that (3) attempts to find an open spot on the perimeter in case the defender drops off to help on the lob.

If (1) is not open, he/she swings to the ballside and sets up under (4). (5) steps to the point, receives a pass from (2) and reverses the ball to (3), who makes a baseline fake to get open (see Diagram 6-17).

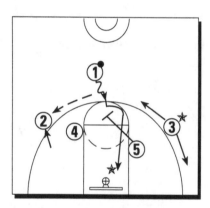

Diagram 6-16: Pre-pattern lob

Diagram 6-17: Reversal into shuffle

(2) may then cut over or under the wall formed by (4) and (1), and the shuffle motion is initiated (see Diagram 6-18).

Diagram 6-18: Over-or-under shuffle

This pre-pattern lob play often provides enough variation to temporarily distract the shuffle pattern defenders.

PRESSURE RELIEVERS

When (1) is having difficulty initiating the shuffle pattern with a pass to a wing, one of the following dribble entries may be added.

The Dribble-Entry Perimeter Rotation
In Diagram 6-19, (1) dribbles at (2) and clears this wing low across the lane to the offside-wing area. At the same time, (3) comes to the point and (5) moves across the lane to set up under (4).

(1) then reverses the ball to (2) via (3), and the shuffle motion is initiated (see Diagram 6-20).

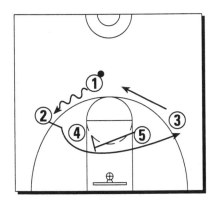

Diagram 6-19: Dribble entry-rotation

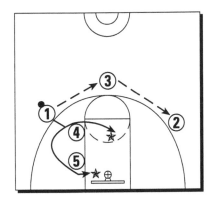

Diagram 6-20: Over-and-under shuffle

The Dribble-Entry Wing Loop

In Diagram 6-21, (1) dribbles at (2) and clears him/her down and around (4) and (5) (who has cut to the ballside to set up under (4)).

(1) reverses the ball to (3) via (2), and the shuffle pattern is run (see Diagram 6-22).

Diagram 6-21: Dribble entry-loop

Diagram 6-22: Over-and-under shuffle

Another option that works well with this method of entry is to, upon the dribble entry, have the ballside post (4) drop low and post up, and the offside post (5) break high as (2) loops to the point (see Diagram 6-23).

(1) attempts to get the ball to (4). If (4) is not open because the defender is fronting, (1) can pass to (5), who may have the proper angle to get the ball inside to (4) on a seal move (see Diagram 6-24).

Diagram 6-23: High-low post cuts

Diagram 6-24: Swing and post seal

If this post option does not develop, (1) passes to (2), who reverses it to (3) as (5) adjusts position for The Over or Under Shuffle Pattern (see Diagram 6-25).

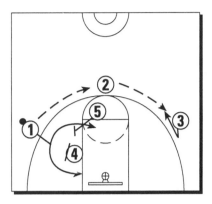

Diagram 6-25: Over-or-under shuffle

PRESSURE ON THE BALL REVERSAL

The Comeback Play

This play is used when the opposition is denying the wing to point pass. In Diagram 6-26, (2) is attempting to pass to (5) at the point, but cannot do so due to defensive pressure from X5. Seeing this, the offside wing (1) hustles over and screens for (5), who cuts away to the three-point area. (1) rolls to the basket for a possible lob pass, and (5) cuts back to the point.

If (1) is not open, (2) passes to (5) at the point, who reverses the ball to (1) cutting to the wing. The shuffle pattern is then in motion (see Diagram 6-27).

Diagram 6-26: Point flare cut

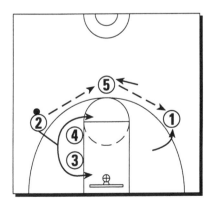

Diagram 6-27: Over-or-under shuffle

COACHING TIPS FOR THE OVER-OR-UNDER SHUFFLE/UCLA PLAY MIX

If a team decides to run the shuffle and the UCLA plays as an offense, the first question is "how strong is our post?" If the post is strong, he/she can be kept in the post by having the first shuffle cutters go to the side of the wall opposite the post. If lacking skills, the post can, at times, become part of the shuffle perimeter by allowing the first cutter to cut to either side of the wall.

The next decision is in regard to the number of times the shuffle is run proportionate to the number of times the UCLA plays are run. The answer is found in the relative strengths of the team's inside and outside games. The UCLA plays are more inside-oriented. If the team's inside and outside games are evenly balanced, the ratio may be determined by the strengths and weaknesses of the next opponent on the schedule.

Another factor that should be considered is the phase of the game that is in progress during any given game. During the main body of the game, they should be run according to the pre-determined plan. Then, if the team is protecting a lead, the shuffle should be featured. If the team is trailing and time is running out, the UCLA plays are preferable, stressing the three-point options.

CHAPTER 7

The Double-Down Shuffle

PERSONNEL

The double-down shuffle and its accompanying lob play are designed for a team with mobile players who have all around skills. An additional play is provided for teams with a strong post player.

THE BASIC MOTION DOUBLE DOWN SHUFFLE

The basic offense is run from a 1-3-1 high-low post set that features the shuffle which is keyed by a point-to-wing pass on the high-post side (see Diagram 7-1) and the lob play which is keyed by a point-to-wing pass to the wing on the low-post side (see Diagram 7-2).

Diagram 7-1: Point-wing entry on high-post side

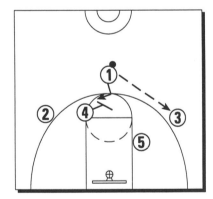

Diagram 7-2: Point-wing entry opposite high post

The Double-Down Shuffle—High Post Side Entry

When (1) passes to (2), the wing on the high-post side, the offside wing (3) cuts below the low post (5) and moves across the lane. (5) steps out to screen on the weakside. At the same time, (1) and (4) join together as they move down to screen for (5). (5) uses the double screen and cuts to the point (see Diagrams 7-3 and 7-4).

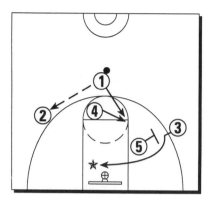

Diagram 7-3: Shuffle cut

Diagram 7-4: Double down

(2) checks (3)'s cut and passes to (5) at the point.

(4) then loops around (1) to the wing and (1), the offside double screener, pops back to the high post position (see Diagram 7-5).

Diagram 7-5: Reversal/reset

(5) reverses the ball to (4) and the pattern may be repeated (see Diagrams 7-6, 7-7 and 7-8).

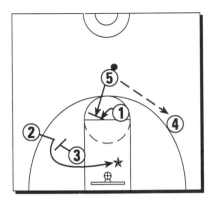

Diagram 7-6: Shuffle cut

Diagram 7-7: Double down

Diagram 7-8: Reset

Note that (5), the outside double screener, popped to the high post.

The Lob Play-Low-Post Side Entry

When the point (1) makes an entry pass to the low-post side, the lob play is run. In Diagram 7-9, (1) passes to (3) and cuts off high post (4), looking for a lob pass.

If (1) is not open, (4) steps over and sets a screen for (2), who fakes a cut inside and cuts to the point. (1) loops to the open wing position (see Diagram 7-10).

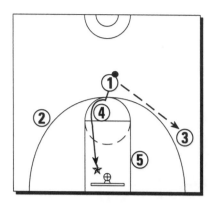

Diagram 7-9: Low post side-lob

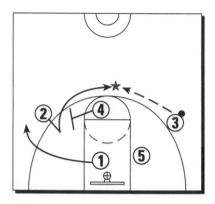

Diagram 7-10: High cut

From there, (2) can pass to (1) and key the double-down shuffle (see Diagram 7-11), or to (3) and repeat the lob play (see Diagram 7-12).

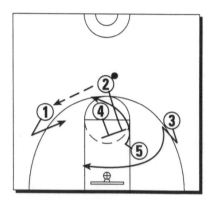

**Diagram 7-11: Shuffle cut-
double down**

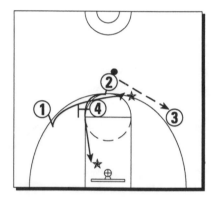

Diagram 7-12: Lob cut

In short, anytime the ball goes to the point, the point may call either of the two plays. This variety makes it much more difficult for the opposition to scout, plan, anticipate, and stop the shuffle pattern.

PATTERN VARIATIONS

As the season progresses, the coach may choose to add one of the following plays:

Screen the Screener
As (1) dribbles into the front court, high-post (4) steps up to screen the defender X1 (1) dribbles off (4), who rolls over a screen set by (5) on (4)'s defender, who hedged

out on (1)'s dribble. (1) stops and can shoot, lob to (4), or bounce pass to (5), who rolled after screening for (4) (see Diagram 7-13).

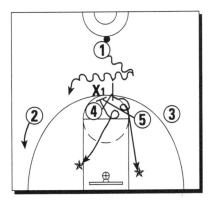

**Diagram 7-13: Double down shuffle-
cut set, screen the sceener option**

If nothing develops, (1) passes to (2) and screens for (2) who dribbles to the point to key a new play sequence. In this case, (5) breaks to the high post and (2) keys the lob play (see Diagrams 7-14 and 7-15).

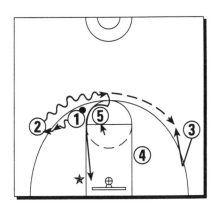

Diagram 7-14: Lob cut

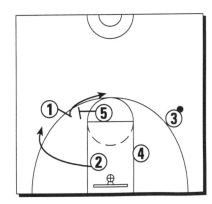

Diagram 7-15: High cut

The Post Play
When the team's post (5) is superior to the defender, the post play may be called. (1) does this by dribbling into the front court and using a key such as holding the non-dribbling hand up with a closed fist. (1) then passes to the wing on the farside from (5). (1) cuts down the lane and exits on (5)'s side. This tells (4) to screen away for (5).

(5) cuts to the ballside and (2) tries to feed the post for a one-on-one play. (3) moves down toward (1) (see Diagram 7-16).

After screening, (4) pops to the point and if (2) cannot get the ball to (5), (2) passes to (4). If (5) had been fronted on the cut across the lane, this change of angles may allow (4) to lob inside to (5) on a post seal move (see Diagram 7-17).

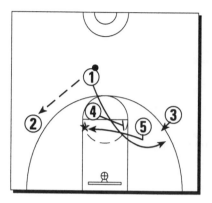

Diagram 7-16

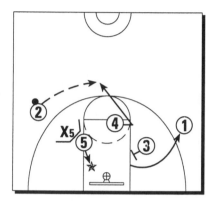

Diagram 7-17: Post seal

If (4) cannot pass to (5), the ball is reversed to (1), and the play is repeated (see Diagrams 7-18 and 7-19).

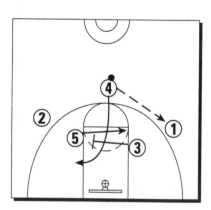

Diagram 7-18: Reversal

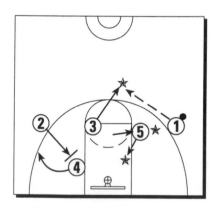

Diagram 7-19: Point through, isolate post

The Three-Point Play

When a three-point shot is desired, a play that starts like Kentucky's Adolph Rupp's old guard-around play may be run. (1) passes to a wing (as to (2) in Diagram 7-20) and makes an outside cut, attempting to run the defender off on (2). (2) quickly passes to post (4) and screens for (3), who has moved to the point.

Diagram 7-20

(1) moves to the corner three-point area, (3) cuts to a point between the wing and point areas, and (2), after screening, pops to the offside area between the wing and the point (see Diagram 7-21).

(4) then pivots to face the basket and either feeds (5) for a one-on-one play, or passes to an open perimeter player whose defender tried to help in the lane (see Diagram 7-22).

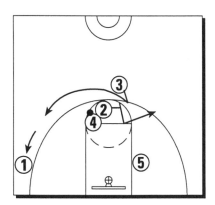

Diagram 7-21: High-post catch and face

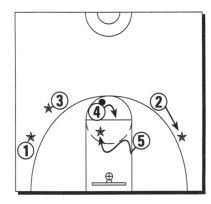

Diagram 7-22: Muscle post and three-point options

The idea of this play is to create a lot of action on the perimeter that spreads the defense and then either go inside for a high-percentage low-post shot or find an open three-point shooter on the perimeter.

PRESSURE RELIEVERS

Dribble-Entry Reverse and Lob

This dribble entry is ideal for the basic offense because it leads directly to either of the two primary plays. When (1) is having difficulty making the initial pass to a wing, a dribble is made at the wing to clear the wing across the lane to the far side. This tells the offside post (5) to screen down for (2) on the cut to the wing, and the offside wing (3) to take the point (see Diagram 7-23).

(1) stops at the wing and reverses the ball to (2) via (3). After (3) passes, (3) cuts off (4), who has moved up to screen. (2) checks (3)'s cut for a possible lob pass (see Diagram 7-24).

Diagram 7-23: Dribble entry

Diagram 7-24: Reverse and lob

If (3) is not open, (4) moves toward (1) to screen. (1) makes a change of direction and cuts to the point, as (3) replaces (1) at the wing (see Diagram 7-25).

Diagram 7-25: High cut to reset

The team is now back in its original pattern set from which (1) may pass to (3) and key the double-down shuffle (see Diagram 7-26) or pass back to (2) and repeat the lob play (see Diagram 7-27).

Diagram 7-26: Shuffle cut-double down

Diagram 7-27: Lob cut

Using this play as the team's primary pressure reliever leads to a smooth entry into the basic offense that is easy to teach and execute.

COACHING TIPS FOR THE DOUBLE-DOWN SHUFFLE

When a team includes a lob pass in its offensive repertoire, it is functional to attempt the pass early in a given game. If it is completed, it has a negative effect on the opponent's defensive plan. Even if it is not completed, they often over-compensate to prepare for it when it is attempted again.

The shuffle is a set pattern, which is another way to say it is repetitious continuity. The fact that this shuffle is accompanied by a lob play helps, but it might be wise to incorporate one of the suggested additional plays that are found in this chapter. A third method is to work out easily keyed, on-the-spot variations. Two examples would be: (a) to have the screener for the first shuffle cutter (see Diagram 7-28) block (3')'s cut underneath and force (3) to V cut back to the wing.

Diagram 7-28: Defense blocks shuffle cut

(5) then backpivots and cuts to the ballside, hoping to catch the defender hedging to stop (5)'s cut. From there, the offense continues (see Diagrams 7-29 and 7-30).

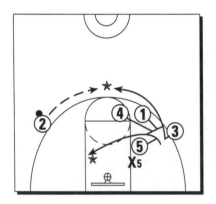

Diagram 7-29: Replacement-push cut

Diagram 7-30: Reset

(b) When the lob play is run and X4, the defender on the high screener, is hedging to stop the cutter ((1) in Diagram 7-31), (1) may cut back to the original point position for a shot.

This tells (4), the high screener, to roll inside of the defender X4 and cut to the basket for a possible lob pass from (3). (see Diagram 7-32).

Diagram 7-31: Lob cut-push replacement

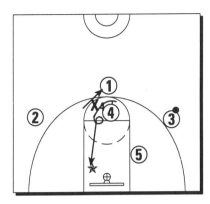

Diagram 7-32: Push cut lob

Many teams have a rule that states "if your offense moves away from the basket to screen, you should step out and hedge on the cutter." These two pattern variations take advantage of this rule. Although they appear to be minor adjustments, they still require practice time that teaches when and how to execute them. They are also essential "counters" to defensive tactics.

CHAPTER 8

The Screen-and-Roll Shuffle

PERSONNEL

This offense is for players who are at their best when they are in motion. In most cases, this is a small team that lacks post-up specialists. It is also effective against teams with tall players who lack defensive mobility. It is used in conjunction with the Princeton plays.

The offense opens up from a double stack with a one-guard front into a 1-4 pattern set. Diagrams 8-1 through 8-3 show three ways this may be done.

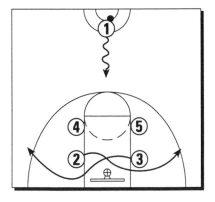

Diagram 8-1: Low cross under

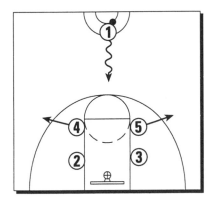

Diagram 8-2: High step out

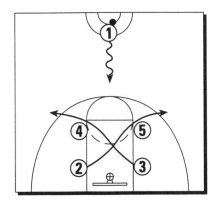

Diagram 8-3: Low cross over high

Note: When running this offense, it is not necessary for a particular player to fill a specific position. This is a five-player continuity with interchangeable positions.

THE BASIC MOTION SCREEN-AND-ROLL SHUFFLE

Using the player positions shown in Diagram 8-3, point (1) initiates the offense with a pass to a wing (as to (3) in Diagram 8-4). Post (4) has anticipated this pass because (1)'s dribble direction was to that side. (4) quickly clears across the lane and cuts under (5) in a path to the wing. (2) cuts over (5) as (4) moves under. (2) cuts directly across to the high post. If (2) is open, (3) should hit (3) when in the middle of the lane and give (2) time to turn the corner to the basket.

(1) comes down, screens for (5), who pops to the point, and (1) rear pivots rolls to the ballside low-post area (see Diagram 8-5).

Diagram 8-4: Point-wing entry

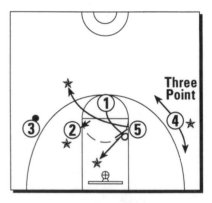

Diagram 8-5: Screen-and-roll shuffle

(3) looks first for (2) at the high post, then for (1) rolling inside to low post, and (5) at the point. All this time, (4) is roaming the three-point area looking for a possible crosscourt-skip pass.

In Diagram 8-6, (3) chooses to pass to (5) at the point and turn the offense over again (see Diagram 8-7).

Diagram 8-6: Reversal

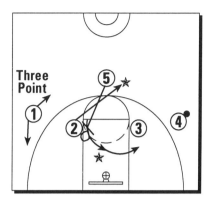

Diagram 8-7: Screen-and-roll shuffle

Variation #1: The Two-Guard Front Princeton Plays

When a coach finds a lack of a point guard who can initiate the one-guard front offense, he/she can switch to a two-one-two offense and use the Princeton plays as entries to the shuffle. Diagram 8-8 shows one of the guards (1) pass to the forward (3), cutting down the lane, and looping around the offside forward (4). This tells the offside guard (2) to slash off high post (5) and to the ballside lay-up area. (5) sets a definite screen on (2)'s defender and then steps out to the point.

(3) passes to (5) and screens down for (2) as (4) screens down for (1) (see Diagram 8-9).

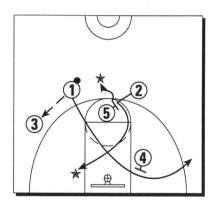

Diagram 8-8: Two-guard entry

Diagram 8-9

(5) pivots to face the basket and passes to either wing (as to (1) in Diagram 8-10). (1) can shoot or attempt to pass inside to (4). Once (4) feels he/she cannot get open, a cut away is made to loop under (3), as (2) cuts over. The shuffle is then in motion (see Diagram 8-11).

Diagram 8-10: Cut away and shuffle cut

Diagram 8-11: Screen-and-roll shuffle

The second Princeton play entry occurs when a guard passes directly to post (5) as shown in Diagram 8-12. (1) cuts down the lane and loops around the offside forward (4). (2) slashes off post (5) to the ballside-post area.

(5) pivots to face the basket, chinning the ball and passes to the open wing ((2) in Diagram 8-13). The wing (2) may shoot, pass inside to the post up screener, or pass crosscourt to the opposite wing for a three-point shot.

Diagram 8-12: High-post entry

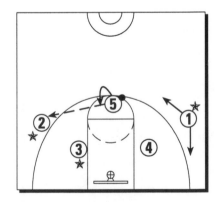

Diagram 8-13: Double popout

In Diagram 8-14, (3) feels no shot is available, so keys the shuffle and the cut by (1) by crossing the lane and looping around (4) (see Diagram 8-14 and 8-15).

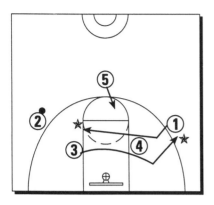

Diagram 8-14: Cut away and shuffle cut

Diagram 8-15: Screen-and-roll shuffle

Note: At this point, a crosscourt wing-to-wing pass may be thrown for a three-point attempt.

These Princeton plays may also be used to obtain a quick shot when you are behind in the score and the game clock is running down, or to kill the clock when you are leading by using them repetitively.

Variation #2: The Stacking Screen-and-Roll Shuffle
When a team wants to feature the double stack with its pop-out jump shots and post-up opportunities along with the screen-and-roll maneuver, they can use the following motion.

As (1) dribbles toward the head of the key, wings (2) and (3) pop out from the downscreens of their respective post players. (1) can pass to either wing (as to (2) in Diagram 8-16).

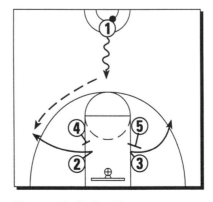

Diagram 8-16: Double popout

(4) posts up and (2) can shoot or get the ball into (4). If neither of these options develops, (4) clears to the low post on the other side of the lane. This tells point (1) to move down and screen for (5), who cuts to the point as (1) rolls to the ballside low-post area. Note that the offside wing (3) did not cut to the ballside high-post area as normally done in the original screen-and-roll shuffle version (see Diagram 8-17).

If (1) is not open, (2) passes to (5) at the point and both screen down for their post players (see Diagram 8-18).

Diagram 8-17: Stack screen-and-roll shuffle

Diagram 8-18: Double popout

From there, (5) may pass to either wing and the pattern is repeated.

This constant stacking and popping to the wings presents an excellent lead-in to a backdoor play. In Diagram 8-19, (3) pops out of (5)'s downscreen and is overplayed on the wing cut. Seeing this, (5) breaks high and receives a bounce pass from (1). (3) backdoors the wing defender, looking for a pass from (5). After passing, (1) cuts around the offside post (4) and (2) uses (1)'s cut and (4)'s screen to move to the point.

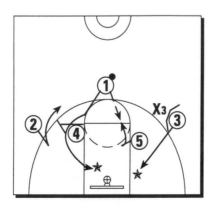

Diagram 8-19: Wing backdoor

To time the cuts of (1) and (3), (3) must backdoor and stop. This allows (1) to be a scoring option. If nothing develops, (4) passes to (2) at the point, who can shoot or restart the motion by passing to a wing. (1) and (3) then cross and assume the wing positions (see Diagram 8-20).

Diagram 8-20: Wings cross to reset

PRESSURE RELIEVERS

The Dribble-Entry Loop
In Diagram 8-21, (1) is having trouble making an entry pass to wing (2), so dribbles at (2) who clears down and around (4) and loops back to the point. (1) then passes to (2).

(2) passes to (3) coming out of (5)'s downscreen. (see Diagram 8-22).

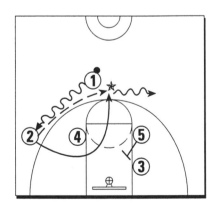

Diagram 8-21: Wing loop clear

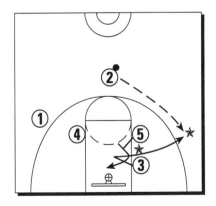

Diagram 8-22: Popout entry

From there, the basic screen-and-roll shuffle pattern may be run (See Diagrams 8-23 and 8-24).

Diagram 8-23: Cut away and shuffle cut

Diagram 8-24: Screen-and-roll shuffle

When The Wing-to-Point Pass is Denied

To turn the offense over, the ball must be reversed wing-to-wing via the point. Diagram 8-25 shows wing (3) attempting to pass to (5) at the point, but X5 is overplaying and denying the pass.

(5) is taught to backdoor the pressure and be replaced at the point by the offside wing (4) (see Diagram 8-26). The ball is then reversed to (5) via (4), and the pattern is completed (see Diagram 8-27).

Diagram 8-25: Wing-to-point denial

Diagram 8-26: Point backdoor on a direct cut, wing replacement

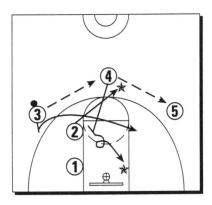

Diagram 8-27: Screen-and-roll shuffle

Another method that may be used to counter "point overplay" is for the offside wing to come to the point and backscreen for (5). (5) cuts to the basket for a possible lob pass and (4) becomes the point after screening, (4) is usually open because the defender will step out and hedge on (5)'s cut. (see Diagrams 8-28 and 8-29). (5) moves to the wing and the pattern is resumed.

Diagram 8-28: Point Denial-screen lob

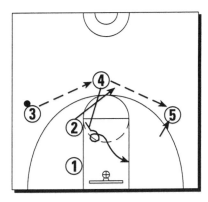

Diagram 8-29: Screen-and-roll shuffle

COACHING TIPS FOR THE SCREEN-AND-ROLL SHUFFLE PATTERN

Priorities
The screen-and-roll phase of this motion is the key element and results in the most baskets. The first cutter who moves horizontally across the lane and the possible crosscourt for three are secondary options. However, if they are used correctly and the team has patience and turns the offense over, they will provide baskets.

Strategically, the shuffle and Princeton plays can be used interchangeably during the main body of the game. When you are trailing and the clock is winding down, the Princeton plays are preferable. When you are protecting a lead and killing the clock, the shuffle or the Princeton plays may be used.

Timing

Once the point has passed to a wing (as to (2) in Diagram 8-30), the post on that side, (4), must "shape up" quickly. If there are problems getting open, (4) should clear across the lane. (This phase should be worked on in practice with the coach telling the post when to clear.) Once the post has cleared, the offside wing must "blow" across the lane parallel to the free-throw line, but be prepared to "turn the corner" if the pass is made.

Diagram 8-30: Cut away and shuffle cut

(1) comes down to screen for (5) once (3) has cleared the lane. (5) should wait until (1) sets the screen before cutting. This will avoid moving screen fouls being called. When setting the screen, (1) should assume a wide stance and pivot (using a rear turn on the baseline pivot foot) to face the ball in the cut to the low post. (2) should look first for (1), so (5) must be sure not to arrive at the point too soon. This may involve hesitating, making changes of direction and pace, and, in some cases, when too soon, making a repeat V cut (see Diagram 8-31).

If (5) still cannot receive the pass from (2), (5) should backdoor the pressure using a direct cut to the basket for a possible lob pass and (4) will replace (5) at the point (see Diagram 8-32).

Diagram 8-31: Screen-and-roll shuffle

Diagram 8-32: Point backdoor— direct cut

Once the ball has been reversed to the opposite wing, the screen-and-roll shuffle pattern is repeated (see Diagrams 8-33 and 8-34).

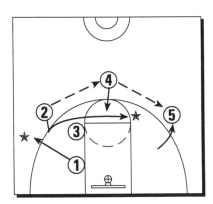

Diagram 8-33: Reversal

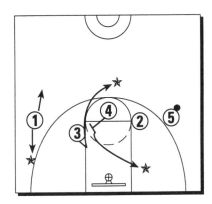

Diagram 8-34: Screen-and-roll shuffle

CHAPTER 9

The "Either-Way" Shuffle

PERSONNEL

This shuffle has a definite three-point option that requires accurate long shooters. Big players (4) and (5) start in the post, but they, too, will play on the perimeter, where they must be adept at passing, cutting, and shooting from the three-point area.

THE BASIC MOTION "EITHER-WAY" SHUFFLE

One of the strengths and weaknesses of most shuffle offenses is that they are repetitive. This makes them predictable and makes it possible for smart defensive players to anticipate and disrupt their motion. A pass is made to one side, followed by a low cut from the offside, and concluded with a downscreen that leads to a cutter to the point. The ball is then reversed and the offense is turned over. The same pattern is then run on the opposite side of the court. This predictability is avoided with the "either-way" shuffle because once the first two cuts have been made and the ball is back at the point, it may be passed to either side. This will determine the side from which the shuffle options will be run. Diagram 9-1 shows point (1) passing to wing (2). This keys the ballside post to clear out by popping to the high post. Then (3), the offside wing, may cut off the post player (5) on that side and to the ballside low-post area. Note that, after screening, (5) pops to the wing to become a three-point option.

(1), who had taken a two-step fake in (2)'s direction, doubles back and cuts off (4) to the offside lay-up area looking for a lob pass (see Diagram 9-2).

Diagram 9-1: Point-wing entry

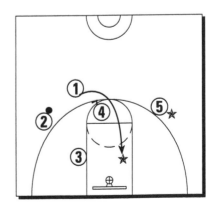
Diagram 9-2: Lob cut

(2) may then pass to the first cutter (3), to (1) with a lob pass, or to (5) crosscourt for a three-point shot. If none of these options is open, (4) steps to the point and receives the ball from (2). At this juncture, most shuffles would require that the ball be reversed to (5) and the same cuts be made from the opposite side. When running the "either-way" shuffle, the player at the point, (4), may pass to either wing and the shuffle cuts repeated. Diagram 9-3 shows (4) pass to (5), and Diagram 9-4 shows (4) pass back to (2). In either case, the shuffle cuts are then run.

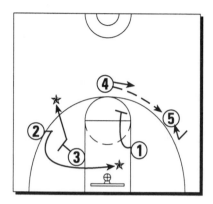

Diagram 9-3: Reversal

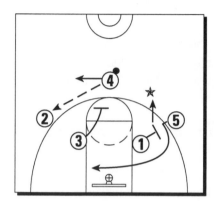

Diagram 9-4: Return pass to same side

Note that the screener for the first cutter always steps out toward the three point line to set the screen. This makes the pop to the perimeter easier and clears the lane for the lob pass receiver.

PATTERN VARIATION

The Comeback Play
In Diagram 9-5, (1) passes to (2), (4) clears high, (3) makes the first cut off (5)'s screen, and (5) pops to the wing.

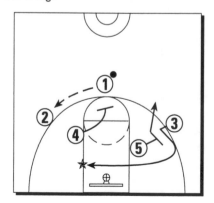

Diagram 9-5: Pass and stay

Note that (1) did not make a two-step fake toward (2). Instead, he/she cut directly at (4) and push cuts (4) down the lane while returning to the point. This V cut tells (4) to rear-pivot and cut sharply to the basket. (4)'s cut is facilitated by the fact that X4 had stepped out to hedge on (1)'s expected cut to the basket over (4) (see Diagram 9-6).

If (4) is not open, (2) passes to (1) at the point, who may shoot or pass to either side and key the shuffle. In Diagram 9-7 (1) passes to (5), (4) cuts high, (3) steps up to screen for (2), who cut across the lane. (1) then cuts off (4) for a possible lob pass as (3) pops to the wing to become the three-point option.

Diagram 9-6: Push cut-replace

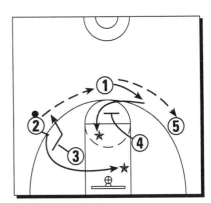

Diagram 9-7: "Either-way" shuffle

The Three-Point Wing Backdoor Play
In Diagram 9-8, (1) dribbles toward the head of the key and (4) breaks up to the high-post area. (1) bounce passes to (4), who pivots to face the basket as (2) backdoors the defender while staying in the three-point area. At the same time, (3) breaks off (5), who steps out, then pops to the three-point area.

If (3), (2), or (5) are not open, (1) cuts over (4), and (2) moves back to the original wing position (see Diagram 9-9).

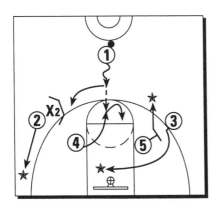

Diagram 9-8: High-post entry

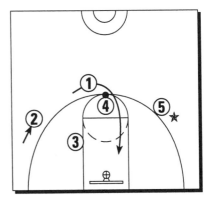

Diagram 9-9: Through cut

From there, (4) can pass to either wing and restart the shuffle motion. In Diagram 9-10, (4) passes to (2) and initiates the basic pattern.

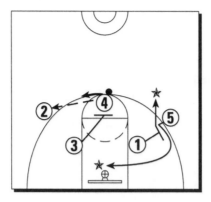

Diagram 9-10: "Either-way" shuffle

PRESSURE RELIEVERS

Dribble-Entry Plays
Since a new play is keyed each time the ball is at the point, these dribble entry plays may be called at that time.

The Screen Away Wide Loop
This play begins when the person at the point, (4) in Diagram 9-11, is having difficulty passing to either wing. When that happens, (4) dribbles at (5) on the wing and clears the wing across the lane to screen for (3), who cuts to the ballside post. (1) moves to the middle of the high-post area.

(5) continues the loop to the point and (1) screens for (5) (see Diagram 9-12).

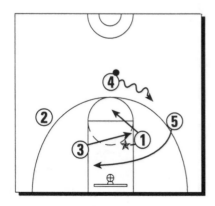

Diagram 9-11: Dribble clear to screen

Diagram 9-12: Loop to point

(4) attempts to get the ball to (3) and if not, passes to (5) at the point, who then can shoot, pass to (3) on a post seal, or pass to/or dribble at a wing to key a new play sequence. In Diagram 9-13, (5) keys the shuffle by passing to (2). This tells (1) to cut high and (4) to make the first cut off (3), who pops to the three-point area.

(5) then cuts off (1) to the offside lay-up area (see Diagram 9-14).

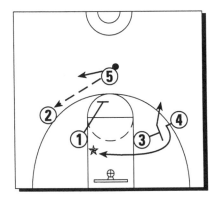

Diagram 9-13: "Either-way" shuffle

Diagram 9-14: Lob cut

(2) may pass inside to (4), pass crosscourt to (3), lob to (5) in the offside lay-up area, or pass to (1) at the point, who can shoot or call a new play sequence.

Screen the Hedger

This play is called by a wing player (2) in Diagram 9-15), who, knowing that (1) has had difficulty passing to either wing, clears across the lane and stops. This type of clearout is the key for the screen-the-hedger play. (1) dribbles to (2)'s vacated wing, as (2) arrives across the lane. (4) cuts across the lane to screen high for (3).

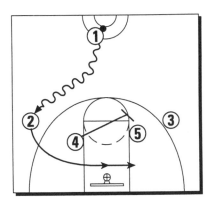

Diagram 9-15: Wing clear and stay

(3) cuts over (4)'s screen to the ballside low-post area and (2) immediately finishes a loop cut to the point (see Diagram 9-16).

If (3) is not open, (1) can lob pass crosscourt to (4), whose hedging defender, X4, was attempting to impede (3)'s cut and was screened by (5) (see Diagram 9-17).

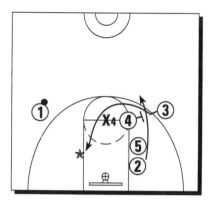

Diagram 9-16: Loop cut and shuffle cut

Diagram 9-17: Flare to corner, screen the hedger

If neither (3) nor (4) is open, (1) passes to (2) at the point, who calls a new play sequence (See Diagram 9-18).

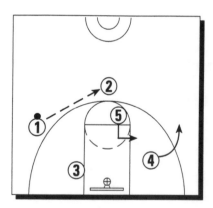

Diagram 9-18: Reset

When this play is run, (1) must maintain the dribble on the dribble clear and (2) should time the long loop cut to arrive at the point when (1) needs a receiver.

COACHING TIPS FOR THE "EITHER-WAY" SHUFFLE

When you are considering using the "either-way" shuffle, you should first determine who will play the positions in the 1-4 pattern set. For example, if (5) is your best pivot player, it might be wise to start (5) at the wing position and place your best shooter (3) in the post on the same side. It should also be remembered that most entry passes are made to the right side (facing the basket). That arrangement would result in (5) being the first cutter (to the post) most often and (3) in position for the most three-point attempts. Over a season, this could amount to a significant difference (see Diagram 9-19).

It would work well to start in a double stack with post players (4) and (5) on top. When you wanted to run an inside-oriented power series where the post players stay inside, the bottom players of the stack would pop to the wings (see Diagram 9-20).

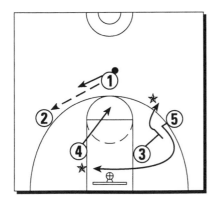

Diagram 9-19

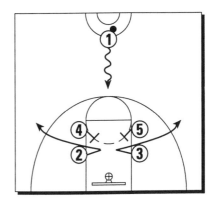

Diagram 9-20: Double popout

Then the shuffle could be keyed when the pivot players pop to the wings from the top of the stack (see Diagram 9-21).

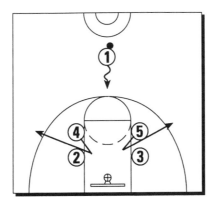

Diagram 9-21: Post popout

Another important point to stress when teaching the "either-way" shuffle is that the crosscourt pass that leads to the three-point shot and the lob pass must be established early to occupy the opposition's help-side defense. This makes the ballside options much more effective by engaging the offside defensive helpers.

The secondary entries (dribble entries and wing back-door) should be run occasionally even in the absence of defensive pressure on the wings. This helps prevent the opposition from developing a defensive rhythm and anticipating passes. Show them a new "picture" to throw them out of sync and prevent defensive anticipation.

CHAPTER 10

Coaching Tips for the Shuffle Offense

PREPARING TO RUN THE SHUFFLE

The following material applies to all shuffle offenses, but when specific examples are used, the "either-way" shuffle of Chapter 9 is used.

General Shuffle Coaching Tips

Successful shuffle teams will face more zone defenses. Opposing coaches may resort to defending the shuffle by going to a zone defense. Therefore, zone offensive practice should not be neglected.

Teams will scout, practice against, and learn to anticipate your pattern. In games, they will attempt to anticipate and intercept your next pass. Your team must break their defensive rhythm by showing them an occasional "new picture" by interjecting pattern variations and pressure relievers.

Good defensive teams will hedge on your cuts, switch on your screens, and double team your point guard. Turn these ploys against them by screening the hedge, running turnbacks or backdooring the switch, and treating a double team like a zone press. Attack pressure.

Don't neglect your fast break. Many pattern teams tend to become one-dimensional. Run the controlled fast break and early offense, and then set up and run a disciplined shuffle pattern with variations. Doing these things well demands much practice time.

Have several ways to start your pattern that have scoring options of their own. The "either-way" shuffle may be started via a point-to-wing entry, a dribble entry or a pass-to-the-post entry. These variations provide different scoring options and a "new picture" for the defenders.

Many coaches feel that interchangeable continuities, such as shuffles, are easy to fast break against or are even vulnerable to long passes. It is also true that it is difficult for the opposition to organize fast break lanes because when acquiring the ball, the shuffle may have taken their guards inside and their forwards and post player outside. A shuffle team can gain an advantage if they have well-defined rebounding and defensive balance plans. These plans from a 1-4 set, such as the either-way shuffle, may include such rules as having the point guard be the first one back or the offside high player become the first one back. They can also use a "mouse" or permanent safety who never rebounds and goes directly back when a shot is taken. The others rebound, but must beat their particular defender back to the lane.

Make the strengths of the offense and your individual players apparent to the team. This would include such things as stating in practice that:

- "He's a great outside shooter and he's open. Throw the crosscourt pass to him for three."
- "Don't be in a hurry to turn the offense over by passing to the point. It's to our advantage to get the ball inside to Nancy. They can't handle her in the post."
- "Don't force the ball in to Tiny in the post. Get it to him/her when he's cutting or on the perimeter."
- "This week's opponent drops halfway to the ball to jam the post. Let's shoot a lot of threes in practice and hurt them with our crosscourt pass option."

Decide what offensive adjustment do we make:

- To protect a lead and end up with a high-percentage shot?
- When time is running out and we are trailing by twice the number of points as minutes remaining on the clock?

Have a last-second shot that takes advantage of your strengths and the opposition's weaknesses. It might be wise to name it after your opposition; i.e. "The Bobcat, The Grizzly," etc. Then use this term to refer to it when you want it run throughout the game, and especially for the last shot. This avoids trying to make up a play. Draw it on a clipboard and teach it before the occasion arises. If this play is successful, it may be used in future games. Of course, it would always be reviewed in practice.

Make sure your quarterback (1-4 point guard) has the skills and ability to overcome defensive pressure and initiate the pattern by making a key pass or dribble entry. If this type of person is not available, switch to a two-guard front and precede the pattern with the shuffle cross type play. If you use a one-guard front, keep the point sharp by running daily practice drills for him/her. Remember that if the point loses the ball at midcourt, it often results in two points for the opposition.

You must establish a shuffle tempo that is appropriate for your team. In many cases, the shuffle offense is run too fast. The cuts should be preceded by changes of pace and direction. This is followed by a quick cut over the screen and toward the ball. It is concluded with an attempt to gain better balance by slowing down and spreading out. It is then preferable to finish in a jump stop and catch the ball in an all-purpose position that enables the cutter to shoot, pass, or dribble while using either foot as a pivot foot.

Weekly adjustments should be made in accordance with the relative strength of a particular opponent. The best indicator may be the old long game, short game theory. Against a team that lacks physical strength, skills, and/or athletic ability, you should attempt to lengthen the game by increasing the number of play situations that occur. This may be done through pressure defenses, fast breaks, quick-shot plays, three-point shots, and free throws. A short game may be desired when you are facing a talented, highly skilled, physically strong team. This would require many shuffle turnovers, few quick shots, an emphasis on defensive balance and retreat, few fouls, no pressure defense (unless needed late in the game), and a disciplined fast break.

If you have smart players who lack physical strength, you might want to develop a basic style that features a disciplined shuffle and strong defense. This style forces the opposition to play a lot of defense and has the following advantages:

- Teams foul more on defense.

- Teams use more energy on defense.

- High-scoring opponents tend to take bad shots when the opposition controls the game's tempo.

- At the close of a tight game, both teams attempt to set it up and work for high-percentage shots.

- If you have played a disciplined control game all season, you may have an advantage in that instance.

The fast break does not have to be abandoned to utilize this style. However, the options must be well defined.

Regardless of the style of play you decide to use, there will be times when you are forced to play "catch-up" ball, times when you must protect a lead, and times when you can play your chosen style. It is wise to have a plan that includes all three of these tempos. You should practice while using the game clock and scoreboard. As a coach you should then set up game scenarios and have your-team play them out. Some examples would be:

- We're playing a very strong team and we have a three-point lead with two minutes to go. We have the ball.

- We are playing a team with strength comparable to ours. We are trailing by five with two minutes to go. We have the ball.

- It is the beginning of the game. We are playing a very strong team and we want to get control of the game's tempo early in the contest.

The head coach runs the first team and the assistant coach is in charge of the second team. Planning periods are made before each scrimmage with evaluation sessions following.

This tip may be the best tip. Develop defensive drills to cover each phase of your offense and drill your team until the correct reactions become automatic. By doing this, your team will face a tough defense each night in practice and not be surprised or dominated by a team that features tough man-to-man defense.

TIPS TO MAKING THE OFFENSE FUNDAMENTALLY STRONG

Following are some questions you can ask about your man-to-man offense that will help you determine if it is fundamentally strong.

- Does your offense have balance; inside-outside, rebounding, floor spacing, and use all players strengths?

- Have you determined the correct method to execute each component of your offense? Have you drilled and stressed them?

- Are the play keys easy to read and obvious to the players?

- Do you have easy rules to facilitate defensive balance and retreat? For example: Do these rules make it apparent who rebounds and who gets back early? What is your transition plan?

- Does the shuffle motion occupy the offside help?

- Do the outside and inside options complement each other? For example: Do the three-point options call attention to the perimeter and open up the interior, and does your inside threat draw offside help and open up the three-point area?

- If you have a cannon, are you shooting it? For example: If you have an outstanding player, are you fully utilizing that player?

- Do you have the proper personnel alignment? For example: Can the point guard do the job, or should you use a two-guard front for your offensive set?

- Does your offense have enough variety and methods to combat pressure?

- Do you have the proper amount of movement for the personnel on hand. For example, should you add some inside-oriented set plays to complement the shuffle motion?

- With the personnel on hand, how much should the three-point shot be stressed?

PRACTICE TIPS FOR THE SHUFFLE OFFENSE

Practice cuts slowly and properly first, then quickly at game speed. Teach all offensive reactions to varied defensive tactics. Do not have a lot of players standing around doing nothing. Players learn by doing. Use an adequate number of balls and baskets.

- Brief the assistant coaches early and give them a group to coach.

- Teach the individual fundamentals involved in the team techniques and insist on proper execution.

- Use breakdown drills to teach the components of the shuffle.

- Don't forget that repetition is the handmaiden of learning. Give them plenty of "reps." Review what they learned yesterday, teach today's lesson, and preview what will be covered tomorrow.

- Explain why, as well as how.

Half-Court Work

After the breakdown drills, run the pattern one time around with no defense, and then shoot on a certain option. For the "either-way" shuffle, it would be:

- Run the pattern once around and shoot on the first low cut.

- Run the pattern once around and throw the crosscourt pass for three.

- Run the pattern once around and throw the crosscourt pass. The receiver should fake the three-point shot and drive the baseline.

- Run the pattern once around and throw the lob pass.

This is an excellent time to stress tempo, defensive balance, and rebounding. Be specific!

Now teach the primary pressure reliever and run it repetitively with no defense. Tell them the "why" of the pressure relievers.

Add the defense and play a 5-5 game of "shuffle keep away". Each time a team turns the defense over (secondside-reversal), it counts five points, a basket is two points, and a missed shot that is rebounded by the opposition is minus five points. A team keeps the ball until the opposition obtains it. Fifty points win and the bench team gets the ball first.

Full-Court Work

Once you move to full-court scrimmage, do it gradually. Here is a progression that works well.

- Half-court to full court (start on offense, transition to defense).

- Half-court to full court (start on defense, transition to offense)

- Full court, but no fast breaks.

- If the offense scores, they get the ball back (make it-take it).

- If not, the opposition may fast break.

- Full-court scrimmage.

The key at this time is to have short, hard scrimmage periods, preceded by a setting of the scenario by the coach and followed by an evaluation.

ABOUT THE AUTHORS

As the basketball coach at Eastern Montana College (now Montana State University-Billings) for 16 seasons, Mike Harkins' teams won 295 games, 10 NAIA district titles, and 12 conference championships. He also coached four teams in international competition. In 1973 he was head coach of the World Games in Rio de Janeiro. Coach Harkins also served as a Professor of Health, Physical Education and Recreation at Eastern Montana College, where he received the college's award for outstanding achievement in scholarship and creativity. In addition, he was awarded Akron University's Distinguished Alumni Award in 1987. He retired from active coaching in 1976. Harkins currently resides in Billings, Montana with his wife, Grace.

Grace Harkins has been married to Mike Harkins for 51 years. As the longtime wife of a basketball coach, she has been exposed to every aspect of the game. It was this experience that enabled her to play a significant role in the development and preparation of this manuscript.

Jerry Krause has coached basketball at elementary, secondary, college and Olympic developmental levels for over 34 years. He served for 30 years as research chairman for the National Association of Basketball Coaches. Krause has served as President of the NAIA Basketball Coaches Association and also on the Board of Directors of the NABC. He has served the longest tenure (15 years) of anyone on the NCAA Basketball Rules Committee where he was also chairman. He is most respected for his emphasis (books and videos) on the fundamental skills of basketball. Krause is presently Professor of Sport Philosophy in the Department of Physical Education at the United States Military Academy at West Point, New York.